Campaign Grind Booklet

The Ultimate Campaign Playbook

By:
Pedro Diaz

ISBN-13: 978-1543115611
ISBN-10: 1543115616

Contact the Author:

Pedro Diaz
P.O. Box 454351
Miami, FL 33245
pedro@diazcampaigns.com

Dedication

This booklet is dedicated to My wife and my two beautiful daughters. Baby, thank you for being my partner in life and blessing me with our beautiful family. Arabella and Alessia, Daddy loves you more than you can imagine. Everything I do, I do it for you. I hope I make my girls proud. Don't ever let anyone tell you that you cant do something. Always remember, "Impossible is Nothing".

Love,

Daddy

Introduction

So you want to run for office and actually win but don't know where to start?

This journey you want to embark on could be one of the most important, life altering, decisions you can make. You want to make sure you have it all in place before investing endless hours and money into it.

I am not going to try to sell you on anything but instead will give you the facts and strategies that I use to win campaigns and get candidates elected. This isn't a textbook strategy with no practicability whatsoever.

My strategies are time tested and are the product of sound research, experience and a lot of hard work.

This booklet is a self-published and edited booklet so please excuse the simplicity of it and any grammatical errors you may encounter.

Everything in life begins somewhere, and first I want to share where I began. I feel it's important to for you to know where my passion for politics is rooted so you can understand the drive I have behind every move I make in my business.

Immediately after I graduated from high school, I started my own marketing company at the young age of 18. Along with my girlfriend, who is my wife now, we provided marketing, graphic design and printing services for small local businesses. Years passed and we were making great money, so we thought. Any money seems like a lot of money when you are still living with your parents.

I knew though, that the money we were making wasn't going to be enough to finally grow up, buy a house, get married, start a family, and so on. To sum it all up, I just wasn't satisfied with what we were doing, I wanted more. I didn't want to be known as "Pedro, the printer" or "Pedro, the guy who designs websites". Blame it on my ego, I wanted a nicer title than that.

It was at this time that I considered politics. My father was into politics; he ran for local office when I was much younger but unfortunately lost his election. As a young boy, I remember campaigning with him, holding signs and meeting voters. It was always enticing to me, interesting and exciting. After his loss, he volunteered his time helping a "long shot" candidate. This candidate worked hard, day in and day out, and wouldn't take "no" for an answer. That candidate won, and when that happened something inside of me clicked.

At the age of 20, I decided to give it a try, put my hat in the ring for a local commission seat. I was one of 7 candidates, the youngest of them all and the one with the least amount of money. My ideas and strategies looked great on paper and I thought I had it all figured out, I had this and I was going to win.

Unfortunately, my strategies (then) didn't pan out, I lost. It was one of the most humbling yet spirit crushing events of my life. After all the time, energy and money spent on my campaign, I had lost. As I looked around the room of what was supposed to be my "victory party" I will never forget the tired faces of my family and friends that had volunteered so much of their time and efforts to help me. They all had on their yellow shirts with "vote for Pedro" written on them and were sunburnt from all of the time they spent out in the sun with me for the last 9 months. It was all over in an instance and my loss affected them just as much as it affected me.

The next day when I woke up, I felt miserable, my loss had started to sink in. Life does go on though, and mine needed to go on as well. I had to make money, if I wanted to grow up and move on with my life anytime soon. So I had to go back to the drawing board. I had invested the last 9 months of my life completely devoured into my campaign that I completely forgot about my business. My clients had gone elsewhere and there was no work in the pipeline. At that moment I thought to myself, what in the heck am I going to do now?

That's when it clicked, and it all made perfect sense. When I filed to run for office, I was solicited by companies and consultants who wanted to sell me on printing and mailings for my campaign but were charging me ten times what I was charging my clients for the same exact service and product. These political consultants had a niche and the price came with the territory.

Even after my devastating loss, I still had that fire inside of me for politics and campaigns, it never died down. So my first thought was, why don't I mix together my experience of marketing and printing with my love of politics and make it into my new venture. I can do what the other guys who solicited me do but charge a fair price for it.

I started off one campaign at a time, printing yard signs, designing campaign websites, printing and mailing campaign propaganda, etc. But it still didn't feed my hunger. I wanted more. I didn't win my campaign but I learned a lot along the way, and I knew that if I took what I've learned and revised it, I could win a campaign, which I did and still do today.

Fast forward years later till today and here I stand. I have made my mistakes and developed a sound strategy that works. I know what is needed to win and what is a complete waste of time and money. I feel that if I would have had this booklet with so much insight as a young and virgin candidate that my results would have been completely different, so this is why I have decided to share my expertise and knowledge in this booklet with you today.

It's important to know that each campaign is different and there are several factors that come into play when it comes to developing a strategy. I am not saying that if you go line by line, word for word, that you will get elected guaranteed, nothing in life is guaranteed not even tomorrow. But I can assure you that if you follow my guidance, techniques and tips and utilize them correctly, you will significantly increase your chances of winning and getting elected. My booklet is not for the egotistical candidate running for all the wrong reasons. My booklet is for the candidate that wants to make a difference in their community and is willing to work day and night to win.

Deciding to Run

Making the decision to file paperwork and run for office has to be one of the most difficult decisions one can make. You will be entering an area of unknown, which can be scary for many. Just like any new venture, may it be a new job, moving, purchasing a home, you don't really know what you are getting into unless you have done it before. This fear of the unknown can either deter you from actually jumping in and doing it or on the other hand can excite, motivate and drive you even more.

Running for political office is not for the faint of heart. You have to know that you will face multiple hurdles along the way. Many people, especially your opponents, or their supporters, will fabricate or dig up negative and hurtful rumors. They will find the smallest, unrelated and insignificant thing you did 10 years ago and bring it to light. They will broadcast anything and everything they can to take votes away from you and secure it for themselves. Don't be surprised if your opponent spends thousands and thousands of their own campaign and personal dollars to tarnish your name and reputation.

It's imperative that you IGNORE all of this. If any mistake can be made by a candidate, it would be allowing these negative attacks to affect them in any way. I always advise my clients that it's important to stay focused and ignore anything and everything trying to get you off track. If you allow these attacks to get to you then you have succumb yourself to your opponent and might as well call it quits right then and there.

If you want to run for political office, you will also have to know beforehand that you will constantly get turned down. Just like telemarketers get turned down on a daily basis when they are trying to sell products, so will you. You will hear from many people that you have no chance in hell of winning. Voters will shut their doors in your face or threaten to call the police because you are trespassing on their property. Potential donors will tell you no because they have already committed to your opponent. You must embrace this and move forward when it does happen. Let that fuel your desire to win and work even harder.

In addition to the emotional challenges that come with campaigning, physical challenges are just as difficult. Walking door to door, day in and day out is physically exhausting. Attending events after being out in the sun all day is the last thing you want to do. Just like you have to fight through the emotional challenges, you will have to fight through the physical ones as well.

Family support is another essential part of deciding to run for office. Without their support you will find it extremely difficult to do what is needed to win. It is very likely that for 9 months to a year before your election, you will not be present as much as you used to. Making it to your kid's soccer game or ballet recital will be more difficult than ever. Your free time should and will be consumed by your campaign. The reality is that voters want to hear and meet you, not a campaign worker or volunteer, but you. You are the one they will elect to represent them.

If all of the above doesn't in any way deter you from pursuing your dream of being elected into office, then congratulations! You have the very important essentials needed to be what I like to call a "Relentless

Candidate". I would like to be the first to welcome you to the Campaign Grind.

Now What?

So you have the support of your family and have decided that running for office is something that you want to do no matter what the obstacles are and have considered yourself to be a relentless candidate. The next step is to actually start campaigning. Now you are asking yourself, where do I start? Which seat should I run for, and ultimately, do I have a good chance of winning?

Developing an exploratory committee should be the first step. Although an exploratory committee is mainly used by state and federal candidates, I find this committee to be an essential part of any campaign, no matter the size.

What is an exploratory committee?

In a nut shell, your exploratory committee will "test the waters" and see if you are a good fit for the position you are interested in running for. If you don't have a seat in mind, it is their job to research the available seats up for election and decide if it is right for you. Your exploratory committee should be composed of family, friends, high profile leaders and activists.

It will be the job of your committee to make phone calls, meet with other community activists and leaders to see how your name fares in the seat you are considering to run for. One of the last things you want to do (which is the mistake I made when I ran) is to run for a seat that, realistically, you have no chance of winning.

This is the perfect time to bring up my own campaign to show you just how important the exploratory committee is. When I ran, I was very young and naive. I just wanted to run and get elected. I decided to run for my local commission seat because of where I lived. I walked into my city clerk's office, filed my paperwork, paid my fee and was officially a candidate. Not once did I even think to inquire about who my opponent is or, in my case, who my opponents were. After some time, I learned that not only did I have 6 other opponents, but one of those opponents had a very prominent name and would have all of the support. Should I of had an exploratory committee, they would of learned about this beforehand and urged me to reconsider another and more realistic seat to run for.

Your committee should also work on getting your name out in the community and making it known that you will be running for a particular seat. They are responsible for creating a buzz about your candidacy which in turn helps raise your name recognition.

It is imperative that your committee and yourself, try to get other high profile officials and local activists to join your committee. These individuals can be extremely beneficial to your campaign in several ways. They will facilitate support, endorsements and most importantly, help you raise the funds you will need for your campaign. Your committee will also establish credibility and deter a viable candidate from jumping in the race in the last minute.

The reality is, if you want to win, you cannot allow your ego to get in the way. I am in no way saying that you cannot take on a big name or many opponents and win - my firm takes down big names and incumbents all the time. What I want to make known, is that if there is an easier seat, it is always my recommendation to go that route. It takes a lot more money, time and effort to take down a big name or incumbent.

Campaign Structure

So, your exploratory committee has done its research and found a seat that is a great fit for you. You have filed your paperwork, signed on the dotted line and payed your filing fee. You are officially a candidate, congratulations! Now, it's time to get to work, the clock is ticking!

Do you plan on hiring a consultant or do you feel you can do this on your own? This should be your first big decision. Let me tell you the pros and cons of both options.

Political consultants run campaigns for a living. They have already been there and done that. They know the ins and outs of campaigning and can help you save a lot of time and money on things that are not necessarily needed. They already have vendors in place for everything your campaign will need, which will save you a ton of time. Consultants know what voters like to hear, allowing them to come up with amazing messages that win votes. Their methods have already been tested and their strategies are already in place.

All this does come at a cost though, and that cost is not cheap. Speaking on behalf of myself, the fee I charge may seem high at first, but my clients always end up seeing the value in it. Campaigns are time consuming, not only for you but also for the consultant. Your consultant will deal with everything related to your campaign, day in and day out, and this takes A LOT of their time. During campaign season, my wife always complains that I spend 90% of my day running around and on my phone. We all know that time is money. Be prepared to pay a hefty fee to hire a consultant.

A consultant isn't the right fit for you or can't afford one?

Don't worry. It is possible to run and win a campaign on your own. You will have complete control and will be the ultimate decision maker for your campaign.

The downside to running your own campaign, is that it will be more work and you're guaranteed to make mistakes along the way. You will have to take much of your time in meeting with vendors to find the best pricing. You will need to come up with a message and strategy on your own, and just because you live in the district, city, town or village doesn't mean you know the needs of the community. Everything will fall on your shoulders. Time is precious in campaigns. Every moment you aren't shaking a voters hand is time that is lost. Keep this in mind when making your decision.

Whether you hire a consultant or run your own campaign, the next step is to come up with a strategy. Meet with your exploratory committee and develop your plan of action. During this meeting you will need to map out your entire plan from now until Election

Day. Assign roles to everyone involved in your campaign and hold them accountable. This is a team effort and you cannot do this on your own. If you have decided to hire a consultant, let them know what you want them to do, if you want them to handle everything then they will take over from there. If you want them only for a particular part of your campaign, make sure to specify their role in detail.

During this time create a base of volunteers. Your committee and volunteers will be crucial to your campaign. Make sure that all these individuals are committed to you and are available when you need them. Set up mandatory daily or weekly meetings to keep them updated and motivated.

Your plan should include all of the following: Message development, Candidate Branding, Fundraising, Campaign Hustle or as I like to call it, Campaign Grind, Strategy and Election Day logistics.

Message Development

Your Campaign Message will tell the voters why you are running for a particular seat and why they should choose you over your opponents.

Sounds simple, doesn't it?

Well, once again, it is deceptively complicated.

For example, let us start off by saying what a message is not. A campaign message is not a list of ideas and initiatives of what you will do if elected, it is not a list of the issues you will address, and it is not a simple, catchy phrase or slogan. All of these things can be part of a campaign message, depending on whether or not they will persuade voters, but they should not be confused with the message, a simple statement that will be repeated over and over throughout the campaign to persuade your target voters.

The second thing to remember is that voters are being bombarded with information every day. They get news on television and the radio, they get reports at work, they get advertisements all of the time, and they hear that juicy piece of gossip about the neighbor down the street.

Most candidates think that their competition is their opponent, when in reality their competition for the voter's attention is all the other sources of information the voter receive every day. Your campaign message has to break through that thick wall of information.

So, while you and your campaign workers are spending hours and hours, days and days, months and months, thinking about, worrying about, doing something about this campaign, voters will give you a minute or two of their precious time and attention. Use that time wisely. You must not waste it.

Advertising companies understand all of this. That is why they come up with a clear, concise message and spend a lot of money making sure their target audience sees, hears and tastes that message as many times as possible. Your campaign must do the same. You can spend hours and hours writing the most thoughtful position statements and articles, but if the voters throw them away in 15 seconds, if no one reads them, you are wasting your time.

This said, you should have the greatest respect for voters. They can see through an insincere message quicker than the candidate can say it.

What Is a Good Message?

There are a number of criteria that make up a strong message.

A Message Must Be Short

Voters don't have the patience to listen to long-winded messages. It might be plausible during a presidential speech when you must have one but while canvassing and campaigning. If you can't hit the nail on the head for them in two minutes, you will lose them.

Truthful & Credible

Your message needs to come from your values, practices, policies and your history. The message must come from you. It cannot be inconsistent with your background. In addition, your message must be believable; candidates who make unrealistic promises simply add to voter apathy. Voters must believe what you say, both about yourself and what you will do, is true. It is therefore critically important to back up your statements with evidence of experience or knowledge from your personal past. Saying you understand a problem or issue without demonstrating why or how you understand it is a waste of your time and the voters' time.

A Persuasive Message

You must talk about topics that are important to your target audience. These topics will often be problems that voters face every day in their lives, not issues that candidates think are important. Voters are more likely to support candidates that talk to them about their jobs, their children's education or their pension then a candidate that talks about the budget, even though the budget may deal with all of these things. Remember you are trying to convince the voter that you are the best candidate to represent them and persuade them to do something, namely vote for you.

Show Contrast

Voters must make a choice between you and your opponent. You need to make it clear to the voters how you are different from the other candidates in the race by contrasting yourself with them. If every candidate stands for increasing public safety and improving the quality of life, then voters will have no way of making a clear choice. If, on the other hand, you will keep taxes low and your opponents will not, then the voters will have a very clear choice. You must identify your opponent before he or she identifies you.

Clear & Speak To The Heart

Your message must be delivered in language the voters use and understand easily. Too often candidates want to impress the voters with how smart they are, using technical words that either the voters do not understand or have no real meaning for them. You do not want to make the voting public have to work to understand what you are talking about.

Creating a visual image in the minds of voters is much better. Talk about people, things and real life situations to describe abstract ideas, such as "economic policy."

Politics is an emotional business and candidates who appeal to the hearts of voters generally defeat those who appeal to their mind. You must find a way to tie your campaign message to the core values of your voters and make it clear that you understand the problems they face every day.

Repeat

Once your campaign determines what message will persuade your target voters to vote for you, then you must repeat that same message at every opportunity. Voters are not paying attention to your campaign. Just because you say something does not mean they are listening or will remember what you said. For your message to register with the voters, they have to hear the same message many times in many different ways. So, if you change your message, you are only confusing the voters.

Candidate Branding

Once you have researched, developed and finalized a message, now it's time to start putting the pieces together and put together an identity for yourself and your campaign. Your campaign identity or as I like to call it, brand, is another important essential. The same way your message has to be consistent, your brand must be too. Once you finalize your brand, you must not change it because you will cause confusion amongst the voters.

I recommend choosing colors that are clean and modern, stay away from dark and dull colors. If you do not have a consultant, have a graphic designer create a professional "campaign logo" for you. This logo should be clear, easy to read and simple. Rule of thumb is, your logo must be seen from at least 20 feet away and should be easy to remember. Just like with any advertising, you have just a few seconds to capture your audience's attention. If your voters have to squint their eyes to read your name, chances are they will not pay attention to your ads.

The same way your message is designed around the voters you are targeting, your brand should be as well. If you are running in a small blue collar town, you can't portray yourself or your campaign as the rich, snobby and entitled candidate. Your campaign needs to scream humble and you need to be the type of candidate that will roll up his or her sleeves and get to work. If you are running in a big and prominent city, your campaign needs to keep up with the market. You need to be flashy and be prepared to have billboards and signs with your picture all over them.

Fundraising

You have developed a sound message and have a nice and clean brand, now it's time to get to work!

Fundraising is such a crucial part to a political campaign. If you don't have the funds, you will not be able to reach the number of voters you need to win. I'll admit, asking for money is my least favorite part of campaigning. But it is such an important part that I always have to set aside my hatred for it and get it done!

There are people who professionally fundraise for a living. You can hire one of them but be prepared to pay a fee for the monies they collect. And the reality is, you can have the best fundraiser in the world, but if you don't do your part, the money will not come in.

The upside to a fundraiser, they have the access to the donors who always donate and they have their own group of people who they can turn to for donations.

Whether you decide to fundraise on your own or hire a fundraiser, be prepared to pick up the phone and ask for donations. As mentioned before, voters are voting for you and donors are donating to you, not to the volunteer or campaign worker on the phone. You need to put in the work.

One of the best ways to start raising some funds is by asking your family, friends, and colleagues for donations. This will help you "break the ice" and refine your pitch. You would be surprised to learn about the people who do and do not donate.

Another way to ask for funds is to ask voters directly to help you. You may not receive the amounts you would from say a lobbyist, but you will find that if the voters do truly believe in you and your message, they will be willing to dish out a few dollars to help you win. I always tell my clients when it comes to fundraising, the worst that can happen is they say "no".

If you decide to fundraise on your own instead of hiring a professional fundraiser, try to obtain a list of the donors who donated to a previous campaign in your area. You can check with the clerk's office and they should be able to provide you with that information, for the most part, this is public information.

I also recommend setting small and reachable monthly or weekly goals for yourself and your team. Have your Exploratory Committee and volunteers help. Give them each a small goal to reach each month. Have them ask their own family, friends and coworkers for a donation. You would be surprised how much you can get this way.

As I mentioned earlier in the booklet, you cannot be afraid of hearing the word "no" when it comes to fundraising. But do not let that deter you from the main goal, which is raising the necessary funds.

Strategy

This is one of my favorite parts of the campaign process. Developing a strategy that will plow your way to victory is the goal. Just like in any business, you must know your numbers.

You need to know how many registered voters there are and how many of those registered are expected to come out for your election. Keep in mind, you will have a higher voter turnout on Presidential election years than you will on non-Presidential election years.

Once you've gotten that information you need to think of this as a chess match and must be 3-5 steps ahead of your opponent or opponents.

Ask yourself:

How am I going to get the necessary votes to win this election?

How can I get in front of as many people or eyeballs as possible?

Living in the technological era, with resources such as Facebook, YouTube,

Instagram, Twitter, Snapchat and so on, this couldn't be easier.

Your campaign must have a digital strategy along with its ground and pound strategy.

Campaign Hustle

Your consultant should have already given you a clear path to victory. It is your job to walk every single door on the list your consultant provides you with.

Your fundraiser knows how much they need to raise. It is your job to make those calls for your fundraiser to raise money.

One of the most effective ways to persuade voters is to go from house to house, apartment to apartment, door to door, talking to individual voters one at a time.

This way you are able to hear the problems they face, tailor your message to meet their individual concerns and gauge the level of support. Often voters are impressed that a candidate would bother to come meet them and you can gain their support just by making the effort.

Obviously, this is going to be a very time consuming method of voter contact. Depending on the types of neighborhoods you will be walking in, a candidate who is disciplined can talk to approximately 50 voters a night or around 300 voters a week. This is assuming that you canvass for about three hours a night and spend no more than three minutes with each voter (allowing a little bit of time to get from door to door). Now you understand why you have to be able to deliver your message in less than a minute.

Because door to door is so time consuming, there are a number of things you can do to make it more effective and make sure you stay on schedule. Once again, these things require forethought and planning. You may consider adapting these methods to fit your needs.

Voters are more likely to remember a candidate's message if they hear it more than once, so a candidate is more likely to make an impression if they can increase their voter contact at the door from one time to two, three or four times. This can be done by first having the campaign hand deliver or mail a piece of literature to the target voters' homes a week before you walk the neighborhood. The literature would say that you, the candidate, will be passing by next week to speak and meet with then personally. Then, when you personally show up next week, voters will be delighted to know that you kept your promise.

You then walk the neighborhood delivering your message both verbally and through literature that is left with the voter.

Finally, if the campaign is able to keep track of who you talked to and who was missed, your campaign will be able to deliver a follow-up card a week later, stating that you were either happy to have met the voter or sorry to have missed them.

The best way to keep the canvass on schedule is to have a trusted volunteer accompany you as you go door to door. This person is responsible for carrying all the literature, knocking on the doors, and introducing you when someone answers the door. The volunteer then moves on to the next door while you talk to the voter, keeping a record of which doors are answered and which not. If you get tied down with a voter who wants to talk and take a lot of time, it is the volunteer's role to go back and tell you and the voter that you have to keep moving. This way it is the volunteer who plays the role of the "bad guy," if necessary.

Stay Visible

Voters want to see you over and over again. Once you are tired of walking or on a lunch break, print out a calling list and make calls. Try to reach as many voters as many times as possible. If they do not answer, LEAVE A VOICEMAIL.

Once it's too late to walk or make calls, send emails to voters so they see your email first thing when they wake up. You need to be in front of the voters as much as humanly possible.

Candidates with money don't do this. They rely on the shiny mailers and a few automated phone calls.

Out hustling your competition is crucial to any campaign. I know it's a total pain, but it's what's necessary to win.

Like I tell all my clients, I know we're doing a good job when voters tell me, "If you call me one more time, I'm not voting for you". Once we hit that point, we remove the voter from our list and hit them up again a few days before the election.

Be a Relentless Candidate!

Election Day

At this point, you have expended a lot of resources, the day is finally here. Now, you are nervous much like your favorite football team in overtime. Your heart is pumping hard and if you are anything like me, you'd lose your appetite. If you win, well the stress would have been worth it. If you lose, there is a lesson to be learned.

As the candidate you need to be at all the precincts to talk to each voter coming in personally. People love meeting the candidate face to face and receiving a firm handshake. If your district is too big, pick the top 10, top 5 or top 3 precincts and make sure you meet and greet every voter walking in.

After a long day under the blistering sun and meeting voters, the polls close. After months of fundraising, walking and hustling, you now must wait and receive your fate.

That feeling you get once the polls close - it's an indescribable feeling. It's a scary yet exciting feeling mixed together, then comes relief.

Get to your victory party and watch those numbers come in. Regardless of the outcome you have given this your all and learned more about what your capable of doing when you're relentless.

I believe truly that by reading this booklet you have increased your chances of winning and decreased the amount of mistakes you would have made as a candidate.

Keep this booklet with you throughout your campaign for reference.

When you win, please make sure I am the first person you contact.

Call me up or send me an email (pedro@diazcampaigns.com) and say, Pedro, I did it! I won! I'll be so happy for you.

I want to make sure that you get elected. At my firm, we strive to put our clients in the best position to win.

I'd like to thank you for reading this book and I want to be the first to congratulate you on getting elected.